Making It Home

*Real-life stories from
children forced to flee*

With an introduction by
Beverley Naidoo

PUFFIN

PUFFIN BOOKS

Published by the Penguin Group
Penguin Books Ltd, 80 Strand, London WC2R 0RL, England
Penguin Group (USA), Inc., 375 Hudson Street, New York, New York 10014, USA
Penguin Books Australia Ltd, 250 Camberwell Road, Camberwell, Victoria 3124, Australia
Penguin Books Canada Ltd, 10 Alcorn Avenue, Toronto, Ontario, Canada M4V 3B2
Penguin Books India (P) Ltd, 11 Community Centre, Panchsheel Park, New Delhi – 110 017, India
Penguin Group (NZ), cnr Airborne and Rosedale Roads, Albany, Auckland 1310, New Zealand
Penguin Books (South Africa) (Pty) Ltd, 24 Sturdee Avenue, Rosebank 2196, South Africa

Penguin Books Ltd, Registered Offices: 80 Strand, London WC2R 0RL, England

www.penguin.com

First published 2004
1

Some villages mentioned in text omitted from maps due to
lack of reliable cartographic information.

Set in Linotype Sabon
Typeset by Rowland Phototypesetting Ltd, Bury St Edmunds, Suffolk

Made and printed in England by Clays Ltd, St Ives plc

British Library Cataloguing in Publication Data
A CIP catalogue record for this book is available from the British Library

ISBN 0-141-31867-8

'I find it very painful, remembering how my parents were killed in cold blood . . . [illegible] . . . the pain is to cry.' – Joyce, aged fourteen

'I was four when we left . . . [illegible] . . . leaving behind me a nice house I was living in . . . It was next to a mountain, and my aunt and myself used to climb it at sunset, her carrying me on her back.'
– Shirley, aged ten

'We took flight from the war a long time ago . . . Nobody told me why.' – Desaange, aged six

'We came to England because we saw lots of people dying and houses burning down. We were really scared.' – Doruntino, aged ten

Contents

More than 20 million children and their families have been forced to leave their homes to escape from the effects of war in recent years. These are the stories of a few of them.

Introduction by Beverley Naidoo

'Is justice sleeping or is it a dream? If justice is sleeping, who will wake justice up?'

Imagine you were asked these questions. The girl asking the question and everyone else in her school were born as refugees. So were their parents. They have never seen the homeland from which their grandparents were forced to flee. The young people waiting for your answer come from families who have been stateless for at least three generations. How would you reply? This is not just an imaginary exercise. I was asked these questions about justice by sixteen-year-old Rasha at Nuzha School in a desperately poor district of Amman, Jordan. Her family had been living there for over fifty years, across the border from home. She was Palestinian.

Later, the United Nations official who organized my visit to the refugee school told me of his own experience. He too was Palestinian. He had been born in a tent. His parents had lost their home, homeland, livelihood – everything – when they had fled the town of Lydda in the newly created state of

1

Israel shortly after the Second World War. His parents continued to suffer from the shock. He had not had a childhood. To grow up as a refugee, he said, is to feel every pressure of the adult world.

The young people whose tales you will read in *Making It Home* have all had their childhoods cut short through some terrible conflict. They tell their stories in a straightforward, simple way. Don't be deceived. These are not simple stories. Joyce from Sudan tells us that her father, an ambulance driver, was killed when she was four. Her mother, a farmer, and others fled from their village. She tells us about the ambush in two sentences.

'My mother was grabbed, seriously beaten and killed by the rebels. I was beaten too but a woman helped me to escape.'

In the next two sentences she tells how she ran to someone's house that, later, was burnt down by rebels.

'I managed to escape and ran to another household who took me in on condition that I did not stay too long . . .'

I had to stop reading to remind myself that this had been the experience of a four-year-old. I looked for Joyce's picture in the photo collection. I found her looking at the camera – and me – through haunted eyes. Even her fingers seemed

2

tense. I continued reading her story, one dramatic event after another, until I reached her description of her 'new parents' whom she said she was afraid of annoying.

'*I spend all my time doing lots of housework and gardening and have no time for playing. By the end of the day my body is aching and I am exhausted . . .*'

Once again, I had to stop. I tried to read between the lines. Was Joyce now little better than a child slave? My heart sank as I saw the next sentence about her 'foster father'. I read to the end.

'*My greatest wish is to find my relatives and get resettled.*'

Joyce's spirit humbles me. After all her experiences, she still holds on to hope.

Each child in this collection tells a very personal, moving story. Reading them one after the other, however, gives a vivid snapshot of what it is to become a refugee: to have your family uprooted, lose everything and be turned into an outsider.

Many of the children hold on to vivid, happy memories of home. Merci from the Democratic Republic of Congo remembers the games she played with her friends by the river. The smell of pizza in Arizona reminds Shirley of small pieces of bread for breakfast in Burundi. Eqleema,

Muhammad and Nadia all talk about large family homes, green trees and gardens left behind in Afghanistan. Neema from Burundi says:

'*I loved to watch our television . . . we saw that the world was very large, and there was much to know.*'

But the happy memories are sharply cut dead. Neema describes a dangerous journey of escape in which they carried their television until it had to be sold. Thieves, hunger and hostility still threaten her family in their present refugee camp.

'*There is no peace for us here or there. I do not see a solution.*'

Yet, even so, Neema remains determined to get an education and 'to become a teacher or a nurse'. Other children hold on to similar ambitions. Occasionally they are offered friendship and kindness instead of being resented and abused. But what really lights up these stories is the spirit of persevering and being resourceful. Somehow, despite everything, these young people still manage to have dreams.

No one knows how many children in the world are living as refugees, asylum seekers and 'internally displaced people' (see Glossary). The number is certainly in millions . . . many millions. Nearly 140 countries, including our own, have signed

United Nations agreements about the protection of refugees. Yet almost every day, popular newspapers show asylum seekers and refugees as deceitful, cunning people who come here because we are a 'soft touch' and they want to get things for free. Asylum has become a big political issue and politicians want to prove that they are 'tough' by keeping out as many asylum seekers as possible.

You could see similar double standards in attitudes to Jewish refugees before the Second World War. For example, the editor of a widely read newspaper in 1938 wrote about the terrible persecution of Jews in Germany and then went on, 'But just now there is a big influx of foreign Jews into Britain. They are overrunning the country.' (*Sunday Express*, 19 June 1938)

I find today's racism against asylum seekers and refugees very scary. It stops us thinking about our real challenge: how to be tough in reducing wars and conflicts that lead to so much upheaval and misery. Racism also stops us thinking about real human beings. It poisons our humanity. We owe a lot to former refugees who, despite all their sadness and loss, bring in new skills, energy and cultures while learning to survive in a new country.

You can feel that energy to survive in *Making It Home*. Like the teenager Rasha who asked me about justice, these young people challenge us not to blank them out. They challenge us not to look the other way and not to remain silent.

Kosovo

Kosovo is a small, mountainous region in the south-east of Europe. For many years it was a province in the former republic of Yugoslavia and it is one of the poorest areas in Europe. Its population – nearly 2 million people – is 80 per cent Albanian, and they call their home Kosova. Serbs, Roma and other minorities also call Kosovo their home.

Ethnic conflict in the region stretches back through past centuries. During the late 1980s and 1990s, as part of the bloody conflicts in the former Yugoslavia, Serbia, under President Milosevic, started to discriminate and repress the majority Albanian population of Kosovo. As well as being denied proper education, employment or freedom of expression, Albanian Kosovars were beaten, tortured and killed. The violence escalated into open conflict between armed Albanian Kosovar groups and Serbian paramilitary and military forces. And the fighting resulted in over 300,000 people fleeing from their homes into the mountains and neighbouring countries, while Serbian forces started driving out Albanian Kosovars,

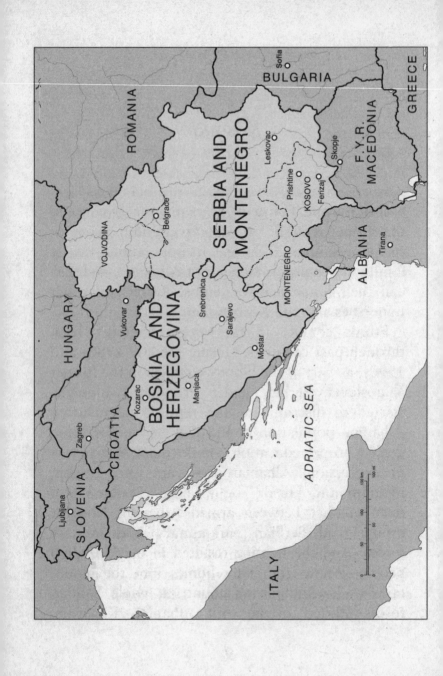

killing families, destroying homes, and blocking humanitarian assistance.

In spring 1999, peace talks in France between the Albanian Kosovars and the Serbian government failed, so an alliance of Western nations, including the UK and the USA, started bombing Serbia. They hoped to stop the Serbs from their campaign of killing and 'ethnic cleansing' Albanian Kosovars. At first, the numbers of Kosovar refugees increased hugely, with hundreds of thousands fleeing their homes and seeking sanctuary in neighbouring countries and elsewhere. But, after several months of bombing, Serbia agreed to a peace deal in June 1999 and withdrew all their forces from Kosovo.

As part of the peace agreement, the United Nations (UN) began administering Kosovo. Thousands of Albanian refugees returned swiftly to their homes, and reconstruction began. But there was also a backlash against Serb communities in Kosovo, and around 200,000 fled from the violence of ethnic Albanians into Serbia, Montenegro and elsewhere. The reconstruction of Kosovo is a difficult task: as well as coping with the loss of family members and many homes being destroyed, Kosovars have to deal with decades of neglect in services such as education and health, and in finding jobs.

Now there is an uneasy peace in Kosovo. There is still violence between Albanian Kosovars and minority Serb, Roma and other communities. This violence and abuse means that minority communities can be trapped in ghettos or forced to flee. It is still being decided whether Kosovo will become an independent country or will remain a part of Serbia, and for the time being it remains a UN-administered province with an unclear future.

Many Albanians who fled from the conflict have no plans to return home permanently. Here is one young girl's story.

MAKING IT HOME

Doruntino is an Albanian Kosovan who lives with her family in West London.

I am ten years old. I left Kosovo when I was four to come and live in England. I live with my mum, my dad, my little sister Rona who's eight and my big sister who's twenty-three and is really pretty. Her name is Arta. We all came to England at the same time.

My home town was called Ferizaj and it is near Prishtine. We used to live in a kind of house that looked like a flat. We had a huge balcony outside. It was a great life. I got to see my grandparents and all the people there that I loved, all the time. There were really good beaches by the river for me to go to, which was quite fun in the summer when Kosovo is very hot, boiling – you hardly needed to wear any clothes. But in winter it was freezing and people don't usually go out because the snow is huge and it lasts for more than a week.

I miss my grandma's house because it was like a villa with beautiful flowers and it smelled really nice, and I miss my grandma and grandpa. I'd really like to go and see them. Right now they're quite poor because their house has been burned down by people who are like police. I heard they are Serbians. They have tanks. They had bad

11

clothes on which I didn't really like. I remember how when they burned a house down nearby, they kept laughing. I have no idea why they burned houses down. I didn't know the people who lived in those houses but my dad would have done. I only have contact with my relatives in Kosovo now by phone.

We came to England because we saw lots of people dying and houses burning down. We were really scared. I don't know a lot about the reasons for the fighting in Kosovo. I'm not sure if there was a reason. I don't think we will go back because the war seemed to last for a very long time. I had to leave clothes, my favourite toys that I used to sleep with, and photos, although I took one photo of my family to remember them with.

When I came to England I felt more calm but also embarrassed because there were lots of different people at the airport – more people than there are in the whole of Kosovo. But I got used to it. In England I feel quite safe and happy because I've got lots of people to talk to, schools that teach you a lot and it's got more people.

I first went to school about two months after arriving in England. On my first day at school I felt shy but it was quite good. I felt excited and scared at the same time. I didn't speak English when I first came and it took me quite a while to learn it from my teachers and friends. To start with, I didn't understand a word the others were saying, so I didn't do much work on the first day – all I had to do was listen. It was quite boring. But I got used to it and started learning. Sometimes I had special English lessons. Now, my friends think of me as English, although they know that I'm Kosovan because I've told them.

I was too young to go to school in Kosovo, but I remember when my cousin took me to a secondary school there. It's not like English schools. They don't have artwork put up on the walls. They have slightly bigger boards than we have in England but they only have one, not two or three. In Kosovo, if you don't do your homework you get slapped with a ruler, not like England. In England they only ever shout at you. And in England the kids can be naughty, but in Kosovo everyone has to be quiet all the time.

We used to live in Slough, outside London, but there were these stupid boys, teenagers, who threw stones at us. Our windows were broken lots of times. We contacted the police, but the boys did not stop so we had to move here. We had a really big garden there, more like Kosovo, but here we only have a small flat and no garden.

13

In England, we eat mainly English food, but we also eat Kosovan food such as *pite*, which is a Kosovan pastry dish. We also drink Kosovan tea a lot, which tastes nice with lemon.

I've got hobbies like telling secrets to my friends and stuff like that, and sometimes playing basketball and sports. I'd like to be a model when I'm older, and an actor. I do lots of acting at school. I also write lots of poems – I've got a book where I write stories about people. There's lots of action. Some are thrillers. I have them all in my head. I started to do that when I was six and I still have the same book. My cousin gave it to me. I also write sad stories of people crying and things like that.

I find England a bit more interesting than Kosovo because it has got more places. Here, people can go out whenever they want, do whatever they want. They've got more shops here. I would like to live in England when I'm older, but I would also like to see my generation in Kosovo one more time. I don't have much contact with my family in Kosovo at the moment. I would like the fighting to stop because then Kosovo would be just like England. Or I would like it if the war had never happened. If the war had never happened, we would probably not have left, but it's good that we got to see England.

Bosnia

The war in Bosnia-Herzegovina during the 1990s was Europe's worst conflict since the Second World War. The four-year war led to the displacement of millions of people, and the deaths of over 200,000 civilians.

Bosnia-Herzegovina (Bosnia for short) had been one of six republics that made up Yugoslavia. Geographically, it is positioned right at the heart of Yugoslavia, and ethnically it is very mixed. The main ethnic groups are the 'Bosniaks' (who tend to be Muslim), Serbs and Croats. They all speak the same language and, before the war, inter-marriage between the groups was common.

At the beginning of the 1990s, the weakening of Communist Party control in Yugoslavia led to widespread calls for independence in a number of the republics, especially Slovenia and Croatia. The Serbian-dominated government of Yugoslavia, under the control of Slobodan Milosevic, resisted these calls, using force to try to keep Yugoslavia as one nation.

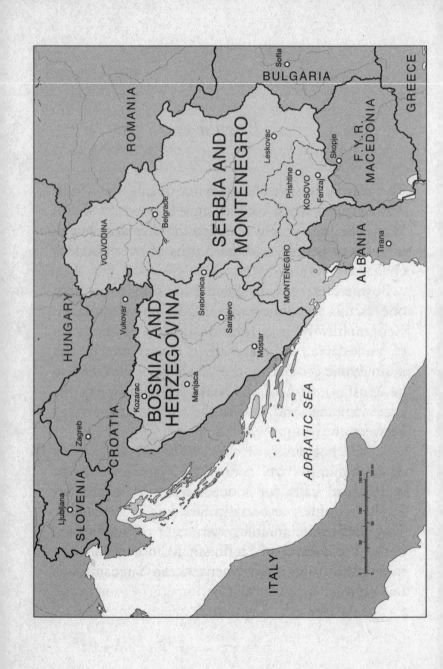

In March 1992, Bosnia also voted for independence, a move opposed by the Serbian majority. One month later, an independence rally in the Bosnian capital, Sarajevo, ended violently, marking the beginning of a war that deliberately targeted civilians. Bosnian Serb forces, backed by the (largely Serb) Yugoslav National Army, surrounded Sarajevo in a siege that lasted until September 1995.

During the four-year war, atrocities reminiscent of those committed during the Second World War took place, with prisoners starving in concentration camps and the systematic rape and massacre of civilians. Bosnian Serb extremists and paramilitaries drove millions of people from their homes in a systematic campaign of murder, violence and destruction that went from village to village, killing over 200,000 Bosnians. They called this 'ethnic cleansing'.

In August 1995 an alliance of Western states used air strikes on Bosnian Serb forces around Sarajevo to end the siege. US-sponsored peace talks then secured an agreement that ended the war and called for a single state split into two 'entities': a Muslim-Croat Federation and a Bosnian Serb republic – each with its own government, parliament, military and police. There is also a national government for all Bosnia-Herzegovina, and a collective presidency

17

with three members, one each for the Bosniaks, Bosnian Serbs and Bosnian Croats.

In the last ten years, a massive international security and reconstruction effort has seen the return of nearly two-thirds of the people who were forced from their homes. The huge destruction caused by the war – homes, schools, hospitals, roads, water, gas and electricity lines – has been alleviated by rebuilding. Yet some are still afraid to return to their homes because of the lack of security, of opportunity, and of access to public services. Corruption and criminality remain problems and the economy is very fragile, with high unemployment. A NATO-led international security force remains necessary to keep the peace. A recent UN survey found that almost two-thirds of Bosnia's young people want to leave their country. Here is the story of one Bosnian girl whose mother left just before she was born.

Victoria Amina was one of the first Bosnian children to be born in the UK after the civil war. Her family is from Kozarac in north-west Bosnia-Herzegovina. During the war, her father was captured by Bosnian Serbs and held in camps in Keraterm and Manjaca. Her mother was pregnant with her at the time and became a refugee in the UK. The family now live together in Luton, England.

My mum was pregnant with me when she came to England. Ten days after she arrived, she had me.

My parents came here because of the war. My mum had to come by herself because my dad was being kept in a refugee prison camp by Serbians. My mum came with my auntie, who had two daughters. My uncle was also being kept in a refugee camp. About two months later, my mum sent a letter with the Red Cross to tell my father I had been born, but she wasn't sure if he had got it or not until he came to England.

When she first came here, Mum was scared and upset. She had a house just up the road that she shared with her sister-in-law and their families. It was a really full house. They didn't have any money and didn't know English. There was a man who helped them and a woman who let my mum into her house when she didn't have any money. Everybody was really supportive, but the language barrier held them back. They couldn't really talk to anyone or tell them what they needed – they had to draw pictures on pieces of paper to communicate.

I'm definitely Bosnian – if anyone asked me, I would say that I was Bosnian. I speak Bosnian at home. It's my first language. At home, we eat a mixture of English food, like chips, and Bosnian food, like Bosnian soup. We go to Bosnia every year. We went for New Year as well. We go there as much as possible. We've got a house there which we rebuilt on the same foundations as the one that my parents had before they left. During the war my dad had been painting the nursery and getting everything ready for me, but the house got knocked down while he was in the refugee camp.

When I grow up I'm going to go to Bosnia and have a house myself. My sister would love to go there too, but I'm not quite sure about my brother because he's worried about missing his friends. The advantage of Bosnia is that I can go wherever I want there, but here it's more limited. I can't really go to a lot of places without my friends, but over there I can just roam about. It's definitely less dangerous in Bosnia. In Bosnia we can all hang out as a family. There is more freedom.

Our house in Bosnia has only got two bedrooms. We've got two bunk beds in the children's bedroom. Dad used to be so popular when he was younger and he has loads and loads of friends who are always coming over, so the house gets really, really crowded. Around the house, it used to be grass, grass and more grass. But now families have started moving over there and building new houses. All our family is just next door – aunties, uncles, friends of my dad. It's good. I get up every morning and go to my cousin's house and we just go somewhere without having to tell my parents. In the summer, it's just really sunny and hot and we go to the local swimming pool. In winter, it's really packed with snow up to our knees. Not a lot of people go to Bosnia in the winter. I don't know any English people who have been on holiday in Bosnia.

Most of my friends are from England. They think of me as English, but they know I'm Bosnian. I used to get bullied a bit because of being Bosnian. I used to feel that I was treated differently because I would get muddled up speaking half English, half Bosnian. But I don't think people treat me differently now.

My parents are happy here because they've made lots of friends. All our family live round here, just

21

a few minutes' walk away. Gran and Grandad also live here – I think they came two years after we arrived. But there has been talk between Mum and Dad that we could be moving to Austria, which is about three hours from Bosnia. From Luton it usually takes two days to get to Bosnia by car. Like Bosnia, there would be more freedom in Austria, and also my parents could get better jobs. The houses there are cheap as well.

I don't know much about the Bosnian war, but slowly I'm learning about it from Bosnian school in Luton. I go there every Saturday. It's a place where Mum works. About twenty people go there at the most, although I think there's quite a lot of Bosnians in Luton. Bosnian school happens all over the country. Once a year all the schools get together. It's good fun. We read poems, draw pictures of our view of Bosnia and things like that, and we have races and tugs of war. We also look at maps or sing songs. It's a bit like an English school really, but it only lasts for two hours. All of the people at Bosnian school are my family – cousins and things. After Bosnian school, I go to a dance, drama and acting club where Mum also works. I'd like to be an actress.

Afghanistan

Afghanistan is a large, rugged and mountainous country sandwiched between Central Asia, the Middle East and the Indian subcontinent. Historically, its position on major trade routes, such as the ancient 'Silk Road', has made it a strategic target for rival powers, and throughout its modern history it has been a site of conflict.

In the nineteenth century it was the centre of the so-called 'Great Game', where Imperial Russia and the British Empire in India competed for power and influence in the region. During the twentieth century it was used as a 'buffer zone' between the Communist Soviet Union and the non-Communist states of South Asia. In 1979, thousands of Soviet troops invaded the country to support a pro-Communist government there. In response, the USA financed the *Mujahadeen*, Islamic warriors who were committed to defeating the invaders. That conflict caused hundreds of thousands of Afghans to flee to neighbouring Pakistan and Iran. By the end of the 1980s, more than 5 million Afghans were living in exile.

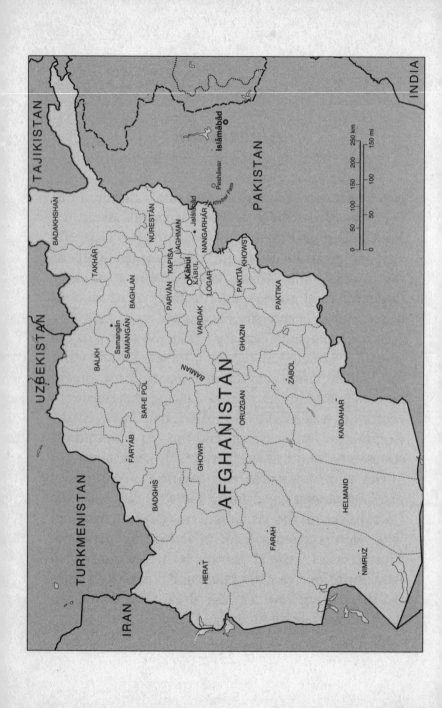

When the Soviet forces withdrew in 1989, the outside world started to lose interest in Afghanistan. However, the civil war continued as rival factions within the country vied for the control of resources and trade in the area. Fierce fighting between warlords reduced cities and villages across the country to rubble, and forced more people to flee their homes.

Towards the end of the 1990s, a group called the *Taliban* rose to dominance, eventually taking control of about 90 per cent of the country. The *Taliban* were originally a group of Islamic scholars, many of whom had fought as *Mujahadeen* against the Soviets. Although they brought some stability to much of the country, their extreme version of Islam granted very little freedom to ordinary people. In particular, women were often denied education, as well as many basic freedoms. Afghanistan was also beset by the worst drought in living memory, further devastating agriculture, the livelihood of most Afghans.

After the terrorist attacks on New York and Washington on 11 September 2001, the USA accused the *Taliban* of protecting Osama bin Laden, the leader of *al Qaeda* and the man thought to have masterminded the 9/11 attacks. When the *Taliban* refused to hand bin Laden over to the Americans, the USA formed an alliance with Afghan groups opposed to *Taliban* rule and launched a war against them. US air strikes against targets of the *Taliban* and *al Qaeda* in Afghanistan left many towns in ruins, thousands homeless and caused another 200,000 to take refuge in Pakistan.

A new Afghan Interim Authority was sworn in in December 2001, increasing humanitarian access to the country and beginning the process of recovery. In June 2002, Hamid Karzai was elected president of a two-year transitional government by Afghanistan's *loya jirga* (grand council). In the following year, an estimated 1.6 million Afghan refugees returned from Pakistan and Iran, bolstered by the prospect of peace under the new Karzai administration and by pledges of extensive assistance from the international community.

However, reconstruction needs in Afghanistan are daunting. Afghans returning to their communities are finding catastrophic devastation from both war and drought. Their homes have been destroyed, their communities have no services, there are few employment or educational opportunities, farmlands are withered, and available humanitarian assistance falls far short of needs. Moreover, security remains far from guaranteed as infighting between local commanders over power and territory continues.

But many still live as refugees, fearful of returning to a country seldom free from conflict.

Eqleema is eleven years old. Her family are Afghan refugees now living in Pakistan, where she was born.

My father was killed during the war, before I was born. I have seen his picture. We have only one picture of him and that is with my uncle, who lives far away. He wouldn't give it to us because he said it made my grandma cry. My uncle lost his leg and an arm in the bomb that killed my father. There are eight people, including myself, in our family.

My family is from Kunar Province in Afghanistan and my elder brothers and sisters were born there. But I was born here in Pakistan. My mother and sisters have told me all about our family home. We had a big house near the mountains and the land was very green, with lots of trees. Sometimes I ask my mother why they left our country. She replies that they would have killed us, like they killed my father, if we had stayed. Now we live in a small mud hut with my two uncles. It only has three rooms, and one of them is my mother's and my sisters'. When it rains our whole house gets muddy. It's very cold here in the winter and very hot in the summer – we can't go outside on a summer afternoon because it's burning, so we all enjoy cold weather.

My mother says children who play on the streets use bad words, so we're not allowed to play with the children outside our home. However, I have friends at the school. My best friends are Salma and Roya, both of whom are my age. We all study in the same class. During the school break we like skipping, which is our favourite game. We also like to study together and solve each other's problems in the lessons.

My day starts with a look at the wall clock. I get up at 6.30, wash, brush my teeth and perform my prayers. If there is time I do some exercise before eating my breakfast. Then my sister and I walk to school together. We have to walk quickly to get to school before the bell rings at 8.00. We line up in the school each morning and our teachers tell us different things. Later, the pupils read articles and poems together.

In school we sit on the floor. Our teachers always encourage us to keep our classroom and home clean. Every day two students are responsible for organizing and cleaning the classroom. Our teachers also emphasize that we should keep ourselves clean. Our health teacher told us that children who don't brush their teeth every day get sick. She also told us that we should eat all kinds of food in order to stay healthy.

I like coming to school every day and enjoy being with my friends in the classroom. There are thirty-three students in our class. Our teachers are friendly and our subjects are interesting. My favourite subject is Afghan history. It has a lot of good stories about what happened in the past in Afghanistan. They are good lessons for us. At the end of each story our history teacher asks us to recall the lesson we learned from the story so we can avoid repeating the mistakes our ancestors made in the past.

Our school time ends at midday. When I go home I eat my lunch then say my afternoon prayers and do my homework. My elder sisters often help me. Sometimes I help my mother with work around the house when my elder sisters are not at home. We all keep our room clean and tidy. After my homework I go to learn tailoring. I am learning how to make clothes. When I am able to make beautiful dresses I will make one for my mother and for me. When my tailoring class is over, in the evening I go to my uncle's room to watch television. I like cartoons and some other shows for children. They show a few cartoons and children's programmes on television.

My mother usually cooks rice. I like it. But I like beans more. On Fridays, when we are off from school, my mum cooks rice with beans because my other brothers and sisters like it too.

One of the happiest memories of my life is when we went to Kabul for our uncle's wedding, five years ago. I was so excited about seeing my country for the first time. We packed our clothes a week before we were due to leave because we couldn't wait for the day to arrive. It was July and it rained on that day. I like rain in the summer. We were all very happy. My uncle brought a huge car and we all got in. It was a six-hour journey. We saw a lot of beautiful scenery on the way. We celebrated the wedding and met a lot of relatives. When we were coming back, my grandma died. We all cried a lot. Then my uncles buried her. I still remember that day. It was the saddest day in my life. I still miss my grandma. My mother says Grandma must be happy now because she has joined my father.

My biggest wish in life is that we return to our country and stay there forever.

Muhammad Masoom is ten years old. He lives in Zakhil Refugee Camp in Pakistan.

There are nine people, including myself, in my family. There is my father, my mother, two sisters and four brothers. My father is a labourer. He works all day long and he comes home late at night. He is always too tired when he returns home from work. He loves us a lot. My mother is a housewife. She is always busy doing chores around the house. She is very kind and she never gets angry at us. One of my brothers is a student in grade eight of Omar Farooq School in the same camp. He works very hard because he wants to be top of the class. Another brother works in a workshop, repairing old cars. My sisters studied in the school where I am studying until they were eleven. They are at home now because there is no secondary school for girls close to our house.

I am from Logar, one of the provinces of Afghanistan. I was born in Peshawar in Pakistan but my elder brother and sister were born in Afghanistan. My father has told me that our family house in Logar had four rooms and they were all large and airy. It also had a big green garden. There were only my brother and sister at that time. They shared the house with my uncle, who also had two children. My mother says that the weather in Logar was very nice. It was not always hot. And they had good and kind neighbours.

My family left Afghanistan because of war. My father says their lives were in danger during the war, so they had to go. My mother says they had a lot of problems and difficulties on the way to Peshawar. They walked a long distance.

We live in Zakhil Camp now. Our house has three rooms made of mud, a loo and a small kitchen. It also has a small yard. It is warm and sunny but when it rains everywhere gets dirty. The weather is very hot in the summer and we often get sick. I like cold weather. My mother says it snows in the winter in Afghanistan. It doesn't snow here. I'd like to see snow.

I like going to school because of all the different subjects I learn, like maths, Dari, Holy Quran, geography and English. I love all my teachers because they are kind and they advise us to do good things. My father doesn't want us to waste our time and end up a labourer like him, so he sends us to school to get an education that will help us get a good job in the future. I have lots of friends at school. We are all like brothers. I have two very close friends. One is Malang and the other is Amid. Their houses are near to our house. We all go to school together and we talk a lot on the way and we all play cricket together at weekends. I also like football, but we haven't got a ball to play with.

When I come home, I help with the house chores. My mother sends me to the market nearby to buy bread, tomatoes, potatoes and vegetables. My mother cooks delicious food. She often cooks potatoes. But I like rice and cauliflower. My sisters and brothers also like to eat rice. In the evening I watch television. I like watching dramas. I read *Rangeen Kaman* [Education] magazine which we get from our school. It has interesting and good articles and jokes. Our teacher tells us to read it and write the good points of it in our notebooks.

I have a lot of dreams. But my biggest dream is to be top of my class at school. I also want to become an engineer and work in my country.

MAKING IT HOME

Fourteen-year-old Nadia attends Khadija Kubra, one of the schools run by Afghan refugees for the Afghan children in Tahkal, Peshawar, Pakistan. Tahkal is a crowded area and is not very secure. Afghan refugees have been living in Tahkal since the early 1980s. They are mostly poor people who can't afford to send their children to private schools due to the high fees.

I am from Jalalabad, Afghanistan, but I had to leave with my family when I was seven because of the war. They were killing everyone and our home was unsafe. Then they closed the girls' school down. I can remember having to walk a long way. There were no cars because of fear of bombs.

I liked our house in Jalalabad because we had good neighbours who were all our countrymen, and we helped each other when in trouble. We had a big and green garden. And we could go and walk about without worrying. When we lived in Jalalabad my father used to take us all to the park on New Year's Eve. We played and laughed with each other, ate our favourite food and had a lot of fun. I always miss those times. It is not very enjoyable here.

We live in a simple house now. It has four rooms and a small yard where I play cricket with my

35

brother and cousins at the weekend. Two rooms belong to my uncle and his family. We are not as comfortable as we were in our own house before the war started. Our neighbours are Pakistanis and they don't like us. They react harshly towards Afghan people. We can't walk out of our homes independently because Pakistani people call us names. They tease the girls. They want us to leave their country. My mother always tells us to keep quiet and not to say anything bad in response.

I like watching poetry contests on television. It helps with my own poems. I have written two poems in Pashto, one about education and the other about my teacher. I showed my poems to my Pashto teacher. She liked them very much. She told me to give her any poems I write in the future so that she can help me.

I really enjoy school. I have kind teachers and good classmates. I have made lots of friends here. I like geography because I like learning about the different countries and people.

I have learned how to sew and I would like to learn more so that I can sew some things by myself. Sewing is not as difficult as I thought before learning it. I have also learned a little about making a carpet. I have learned it from one of my classmates. It is really interesting.

I have learned in the school that unity and peace bring all good in a country, so I always pray for peace and unity among our people in our country so that we can return there and continue our education and live there forever.

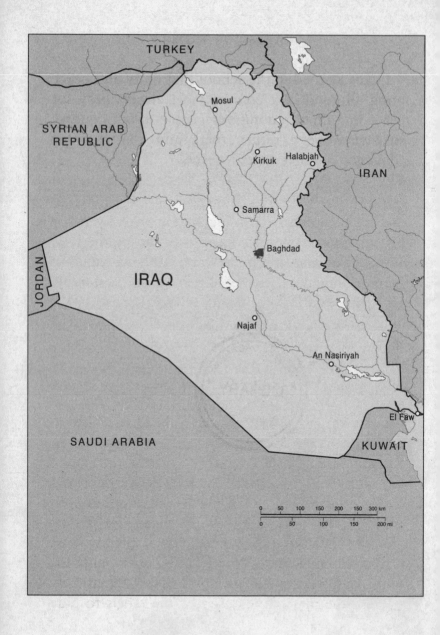

Iraq

The area of Iraq was the cradle of various ancient civilizations. But its location and resources, including oil, have led to it being fought over by many foreign powers. Britain occupied it during the First World War and, after the war, under a League of Nations mandate, helped to install a monarchy. However, Arab nationalism grew during the 1940s and 50s, including Ba'athism that promoted a secular, socialist state. In 1958, the king was overthrown by a military coup. After a series of unstable governments, the Ba'athist party staged a coup and took power in 1968. Saddam Hussein became its leader and President of Iraq in 1979.

Intolerant of any opposition to his leadership, Saddam used brutal means to put it down. Chemical and biological weapons were deployed against the Kurds in the north of the country to suppress the ongoing rebellion there; one attack alone in Halabjah killed thousands of men, women and children. In southern Iraq, a focal point for numerous resistance groups, he systematically drained the marshlands used by the rebels to hide in. The result was the destruction of an environment that the marsh Arabs had depended on for 5,000 years. Political opponents were imprisoned, tortured and frequently killed.

The two major wars during his regime – the Iran–Iraq War and the Gulf War – together with sanctions imposed by the international community combined to devastate Iraq's economy and society. Many Iraqis left their homes rather than endure the hardship Saddam's regime imposed. At the beginning of 2002 there were over 400,000 Iraqi refugees living in 90 countries across the world including places as distant and diverse as South Africa, Sri Lanka, America and Argentina. Over half of these, however, were located in just one country: the Islamic Republic of Iran.

Saddam was finally deposed in 2003, following the three-week US-led war. But the country is still struggling with its past, and Iraq's future is by no means secure. A year after coalition forces arrived, civil unrest was rife, and a new political system had yet to be created. The human cost is difficult to calculate.

Here are the stories of three young Iraqis.

Taef Tozy is thirteen years old. He left Iraq with his family in 1998 and is now living as a refugee in San Diego, California, USA.

I was born in Mosul, Iraq, and have wonderful memories of my family and my homeland. But in 1998 my family decided to leave because of the effects of the war. There was little food, and supplies were scarce. My parents wanted their children to have freedom and a better education. We left Iraq when I was only eight years old. It was a confusing time for me. At that age you do not know why things happen. You are playing with your friends one day, and the next day you are saying goodbye to them. I was in shock. The saddest memory I had was saying goodbye to my relations. I realized when I was saying goodbye that this might be my last chance to see the people that I loved. I did not even have the chance to say goodbye to some people. That was very hard. I still remember the sounds of war and planes flying overhead. I was scared.

My father went to Syria to try to make a new life for us while my mother, three brothers and sister and I travelled to Jordan. We did not see my father for six months, until we joined him in Syria. Those were the most difficult months of my life because I missed my father so much.

In Jordan we didn't know anyone. We couldn't leave the house. I didn't get to go to school. For six long months I had no formal education and I hated that. I was sad because I missed the people we left behind. I could no longer spend holidays together with my family left behind in Iraq, and I could no longer play sports with my best friends.

Life was not easy in Jordan and Syria. My older brothers and sister were working to support the family. I do have some fond memories of that time. I used to love playing football in the garage with my brothers – those could be wonderful times. Another great memory was when my sister was married in Syria. After two and one half years of living in Syria, we were able to come to the United States. Everything is different here.

In Iraq there was war. We could hear aeroplanes flying over. Bombs exploded and windows would shake and shatter, even far away. We did not like what was happening to our country. In America we do not hear those things.

I have been in the United States for a year now. Although I knew a little English before, I have learned even more now and am doing really well in school. I love school and the chance to get an education. I still like to play football.

Being a refugee means many things to me. The war broke families apart. The family of the place where you are born is the closest thing that you have in your life. When you leave your country, you still think about the country in your head, and you never forget. You are always back there in your heart. You have a new country, but the old country stays with you.

Martien Audesh is fourteen years old. He and his family are Chaldean Muslims, a persecuted minority in Iraq who were forbidden to practise their religion. Like Taef, Martien is now living in San Diego in the United States with his family.

I was born in Baghdad, Iraq, and left in 1999 when I was only nine years old. My mother and father decided to leave because Iraq was a bad place to live. They wanted a better future for us. We were fleeing from war and from religious persecution.

The worst thing was having to leave my family behind in Iraq. Do you know how really bad it is to leave family and friends behind, knowing you may never see them again? When we left Iraq, we stayed in Jordan for three days before travelling to Greece. I was lucky because I had aunts and uncles who came to Greece with us. My father went ahead to America to start a new life for us all. We did not see him for three years. Those were the worst years of my life. Life without my father was very sad. Even football did not stop my sadness over not seeing my dad.

I left Greece two years ago. Seeing my father again was one of the happiest days of my life. While in Greece, I learned some English and I've learned a lot more here. I have thought about what it means to me to be a refugee. I am a normal child. I like to talk, play sports and have fun. I really like school. In Iraq there was religious fighting. It was hard for the Chaldeans. We did not have religious freedom there, but here in America we can worship as we want.

Life changes when you are a refugee. If you have to leave your family and your friends, you want to cry. You do cry. You always wish to see them again, but you can't. In your imagination you think about these people a lot and you don't forget them or what happened to make you lose them. Being a refugee means separation from the people and things you love.

Azeza Kalaf Ali had to leave her home in the deep south of Iraq when she was five in order to escape from the effects of the Iran–Iraq War.

I am seventeen years old now. I live with my parents, two brothers and four sisters in a deserted school because we don't have our own home any more. We lost it during the Iran–Iraq War when El Faw, where we are from, became a war zone. I can remember the horror of the fighting, rockets falling on our city, buildings being destroyed and people being killed. I saw a man burning on the street because of the bombs. He became like a piece of coal. We decided we had to leave and moved to Najaf in south central Iraq. To start with, we lived with some relatives, but they were poor and could not support us so we moved to a deserted school where we've lived for over twelve years with ten other families. El Faw is like a ghost town now.

I don't have many happy memories. I had to leave school when I was very young, and none of my brothers and sisters (except for Ali, who is eight) have even been to school. I worked as a cleaner in a college for a while, but I don't have a job at the moment – although I'd like to. When I was working I had a routine. I'd go to work, come home for a lunch of bread, rice and vegetables, and then have a sleep. Later, when it's cooler, I'd spend time with my family, chatting and watching television. But these days I spend my time at home and visiting holy places in Najaf.

My biggest wish is to live in a private house with my family. This school is like a prison occupied by ten families. I want to live freely.

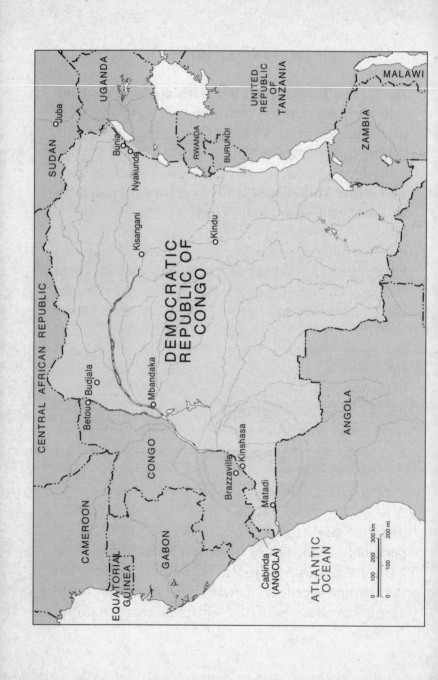

Congo

The Democratic Republic of Congo, which used to be known as Zaïre, is one of the largest and poorest countries in Africa. Over the past 300 years its history has been punctuated by bloodshed and loss. Following the destruction of its society through slavery during the eighteenth and nineteenth centuries, in 1895 it became a Belgian colony under King Leopold II. His regime was brutal. He forced the local people to harvest the lucrative wild rubber, using the cruellest of methods and making a fortune for himself in the process. Up to 10 million people are believed to have died as a direct result of his rule. The country has never recovered, and its immense natural resources – diamonds, tin, copper, timber – have been fought over and exploited since Belgian rule ended in 1960.

Mobutu Sese Seko, the American-backed dictator who ruled from 1965 to 1996, grew personally rich, failing to invest in even the most basic amenities – schools, hospitals, roads – that the people needed. Since 1996 war has raged almost constantly in the DRC as seven nations, three main rebel groups and numerous militias fight with a complicated mixture of economic, ethnic and political motives. Over 3 million people have died since 1998 as a direct result of the recent fighting, and millions more have been forced to leave their homes.

Despite a peace agreement signed by the warring parties in 2003, fighting still continues within the DRC. As of early 2004, the country remained effectively divided into three – the two main rebel factions in the north and the east and the government-controlled territory in the west. People were still fleeing their homes and many refugees have ended up in camps just across the border in the Republic of Congo, a small country without the resources to cope with large numbers of refugees.

Clarisse Kabwiz Tshiyena is fifteen years old. She left the Congo when she was ten in order to escape from the civil war. She now lives in America with her family.

I'm from the Democratic Republic of Congo in Central Africa. My family – my parents, myself, my three sisters, and my cousin – lived in a beautiful home in a big town. We had a very modern house with electricity, water and a telephone. We loved our home, but we had to leave and go to Zambia in 1999 because of the civil war – there was lots of fighting and it wasn't safe to stay in our home any more.

In Zambia we lived in a refugee camp, which was very hard. It's my worst memory. In the Congo everyone spoke French, but in Zambia we had to learn English. It was hard to learn a new language and leave our friends and our home. My sister Evelyne and I are very close. I am the oldest and she is four years younger than me. We played lots of games together when we were growing up. I like to play all kinds of games, but Evelyne likes to race the best. She is very fast and wins lots of races.

We lived in the refugee camp for four years, and then we came to America. Getting on the plane to America and knowing that I would never have to live in the refugee camp again is my favourite memory.

Our family now lives in Phoenix, Arizona. We live in a nice apartment. I share a room with my sister. My parents are both working and are very happy to be living in America. My mother is a tailor and my father works in an office. My mother is teaching me to cook – I eat lots and lots of eggs. Evelyne is learning to cook too, but she doesn't like to eat vegetables. That makes my mother mad!

I like living in Phoenix, but it has been hard getting used to the language and the weather. Evelyne and I both go to the same school, which we love. The teachers have been very nice and have helped us improve our English and we've made lots of new friends. My sister and I were chosen as students of the month for our grades, which made us very proud and happy.

The weather here is very different from Africa. It is too hot in the summer and too cold in the winter, but my sister and I want to stay here forever.

Madeleine Sega is fourteen years old and from the Democratic Republic of Congo. She was separated from her family when she was three or four. She now lives in Betou, in the neighbouring Republic of Congo, and is going to be reunited with her family soon.

My name is Madeleine Sega, but most people call me Mado. When I was three or four years old (I do not remember very well), I left my family in Kinshasa to travel with a close friend of the family. Her name was Mado too. We used to call her Mama Mado in our family. I often travelled with her from Kinshasa in the south to Dongo, a market town in the north of the country. But on one of these trips Mama Mado had some problems and couldn't return to Kinshasa and my family. So I stayed in Dongo with Mama Mado and her husband and her own daughter, who was older than me, for several years. Throughout all that time, I wanted to be back together with my family, even though I did not remember them very well. But I can now see how it could happen.

In Dongo, life was OK. We lived in a house like the one we have now, made of mud and palm-tree leaves. I didn't go to school. Instead I helped Mama

Mado at home with the cooking and made things to sell at the market.

We lived on the edge of the town and I had many friends in the neighbourhood. We played lots of games about being older and having a family. We would use old cans we found in the town and pretend to make meals for each other with them. I have happy memories of setting up obstacles in the water and then draining the water out to catch the fish inside. After that, we would cook the fish over a fire and prepare a big meal for our families. Sometimes my favourite food, mango cut early from the tree and treated with salt, would also be served. The best season for this dish is in February and March.

The work with Mama Mado was hard. We had to make so many things to sell in the market. Some jobs, like grinding, drying and mixing corn to make alcohol, were very heavy work. I prefer not to remember them.

After a few years in Dongo, the war came and there was lots of fighting. People said the military were angry with everyone in the town, so we all went into the forest. I was with a group of people, including Mama Mado's husband. Mama Mado herself had crossed the river to the Republic of Congo a few days before to sell things in a market over there. After a week or two the military began chasing the people hiding in the forest. We stayed in the forest for a month and a half, with little food and water or anything else. One of the men with us was killed by the military during that time.

One night, while most of the military soldiers were in the forest, we travelled back to the town and arranged for some canoes to take us across the river. We crossed in the night and came to a place where many other people from Dongo were staying. It was called Eboko and had been very small before, but now it was full of people, sleeping everywhere with very little shelter. It was there that we found Mama Mado again. She had stayed there during all the trouble, waiting for us to cross the river.

After we were all together again, we travelled south to a bigger town called Boyele Centre. There were a lot of refugees there, but there was a good market and places to stay. In Boyele, we started to rebuild our lives again. It wasn't that different to Dongo. The weather is the same, with a rainy season and a dry season, but warm temperatures almost all the time. We found another mud house to stay in and we all lived together, except for Mado's daughter, who moved away to go to school. I started going to school in Boyele a little, but I still spent most of my time working at home.

After about two years, I began to have more problems with Mama Mado. She began to treat me badly and I was unhappy, so I started staying with other families in Boyele. Sometimes I even slept outside in the market. This went on for a few months until one of the people I stayed with said they thought they knew something about my real family, back in Kinshasa. And now the Red Cross has found my mother's family. I'm staying here in Betou until it's time for me to leave.

I am excited about the changes this may bring to my life but also a little nervous. I do not really remember my family. I don't even know if I have any brothers or sisters. But I'm confident that they will treat me well and I will find happiness back in my own country. I have been a refugee for three years but I have been away from my family for much longer than that.

My biggest wish for the future is to have a husband and a family of my own, and to live in a nice house. And then we will be able to offer a home to my father and other older family members, the way that they are offering a home to me now.

Merci Ngubi is fifteen and comes from the Demo-cratic Republic of Congo. She is currently living in a village community for refugees in the Republic of Congo.

I live in the village of Betou, near the market. Our neighbourhood is a busy place, with lots of people and animals coming and going all the time. My home is made from wooden planks that had been thrown away by a local timber company. I collected the planks with my family until we had enough to build our house. The roof is made from palm-tree leaves and the floor is made from dirt.

I live with seven people: my mother, stepfather, three brothers, uncle and grandmother. My real father left our family many years ago. We have been in Betou for about three years, since the war started near our old home. I like my mother and stepfather. They are both nurses at the hospital in Betou which is managed by a French organization called Médecins Sans Frontières (MSF). We do not know how long MSF will stay here and we do not know what will happen if they leave. My parents might be able to carry on working, or things in the Democratic Republic of Congo might improve enough for us to be able to go home.

I grew up in a town called Budjala, about 400

kilometres away from here. Life was good there. I lived in a mud house there with my family; I went to school and had many friends. My happiest memory is playing with my friends in a small river that was near the town. Many people from the town fished there because during the dry season the fish were easy to catch. Sometimes I helped my family to fish, but mostly I just enjoyed passing the time with my friends. We would play many games together. One game we played is called *Ndzango*. It is a complicated game you play with a partner and with your hands and feet. There is much clapping of hands and moving quickly, and it is quite fun. There is also another game we played called *Bonjour*. For this game you need ropes. It's difficult to learn but I enjoyed it because you can play with many people and do a lot of jumping.

Our typical meal back home was fish with rice or cassava. That has not changed much since coming to Betou. I am lucky that I enjoy this food quite a lot.

Then in July 2000, when I was twelve years old, everything changed. We heard that fighting had broken out between the Democratic Republic of Congo military and the rebel soldiers, less than 30 kilometres away. We knew that the situation was very serious – if the fighting reached the town, we would be in great danger. So we gathered together everything we could carry and left on foot – myself, my family and some other people from the town – and started walking through the forest, away from the fighting. My family decided that the best thing to do was to head for the river so we could cross it and leave DRC. That way we would be sure to be safe.

We walked through the forest together for two weeks, carrying all our belongings on our heads, until we reached the river. Luckily, we didn't run into any fighting along the way. We crossed the river by canoe. When we reached the other side, we arrived in a small village called Malebo. There were other refugees there as well, but we had heard about Betou and that there might be more help and shelter there, so we decided to go.

When we arrived here, we found a nice man in a part of town called Yende, and he agreed to let us stay with him for a while. We worked hard in the first few months to try and make a new home, but it was not easy. We sold peanuts and beignets in the market and started to plan having our own home again. After some time, MSF came to Betou and started rebuilding the local hospital, and my mother and stepfather found work there. Once we'd saved a bit more money, we moved away from Yende because sometimes the local police made trouble for refugees there. Now we live in a neighbourhood called Monzombo, where there are more people and fewer problems.

I go to school in the afternoons, so in the mornings and on the weekends I help the family around the house, washing dishes and clothes, sweeping our house and yard, preparing food and bringing water from the well nearby. I have also made a garden next to our house that I'm very proud of. I am growing tomatoes and onions and manioc for now, but I will change it soon.

One day I would like to be a nurse, like my mother. I would also like to have a family and four children. But I do not know where that will be.

For now, the first thing I see in the morning is my mosquito net and palm-leaf ceiling. This is not so different from in my own country. Maybe we will stay here or maybe we will go back when things get better. I do not know. I will have to think about it.

Desaange Tandichabo is six years old, and her brother Innocent is seven. They come from Nyakunde, a village in Ituri Province, north-eastern Democratic Republic of Congo. They now live in a camp for internally displaced people (IDP), on the outskirts of Bunia, which is home to about 13,000 displaced people. The camp was established in May 2003, when fighting and massacres between the Hema and Lendu ethnic groups in the region increased, leading to people like Desaange and Innocent fleeing from villages threatened by the conflict and converging on a stretch of land next to the UN military base for protection.

We took flight from the war a long time ago. We ran from Nyakunde and came to Kindia [an area of Bunia town]. My grandma and grandpa live in a house in Kindia. But after that we came to the camp. Nobody told me why. My house in Nyakunde was on the edge of the town and was middle-sized. We had three goats there and a little garden for growing rice. We also grew manioc and beans – that is all. I was in the first year at school at Nyakunde and I liked it very much.

In Nyakunde I got up in the morning and went to school, after that I ate something and played, and then washed things for my mother and helped

61

her in the house, played some more and after that would go to sleep early. My brother, Innocent, he liked to play football there. There was a big place to play in, but here in the camp there is nowhere big like that to play. Things were good in Nyakunde.

I have three brothers who now live in Kindia. My other brothers – they are with me here in the camp. One brother in Kindia is called Billon, he is my friend. My mum and dad – they now stay in Kindia and I live in the camp with my big brother and his wife and my other brother, Innocent and a baby.

Here in the camp, I wake up early and the first thing I see is darkness. I share a bed place with Innocent. I get up and wash my face and teeth and then do washing up. After, I relax and eat with Innocent, and then I wash up our dirty things. There is other work to do. I do the beans with Innocent. We take out the bad ones and put the others in a pot. I make the fire go so we can cook them in water. Innocent – he likes the beans very much and eats a lot. Then I sweep the floor and clean things up; and afterwards I play with other children who live nearby.

I play the games of girls, with a ball, or a plastic bag, and then we leave our games because it is time for school with UNICEF in the tent up the hill. There are a lot of children in the school, boys and girls, all mixed up. I am in class one. We are all nearly the same age, but there are also some big people who have never studied and don't know anything. I am learning the vowel 'A' – it is not difficult. At school we don't eat anything, but after school, at home we eat manioc and beans and maize – that is all. Sometimes there is a bit of meat, but not often.

I want to live in Kindia with my mum and dad because I like it very much there, but we must live here in the camp. Nobody tells me why. Our house here is very small and made of plastic and wood. There are five people who live in my house here, my brother Innocent, my big brother, his wife and their baby. And lots of other people live nearby. Now there is a lot more sun than before, and that is good. When it rains a lot, I don't like it because water gets in my house and everything gets wet. Sometimes we get very cold. In Nyakunde that didn't happen. I liked my old house and Nyakunde, and when I think about it I am sad.

My saddest memory is the war. When fighting and shooting started in Nyakunde village, we took flight and my brother was shot with a gun and died in front of me when we were running from our house. He fell down and we left him because we were very scared. I miss him very much. Sometimes at night we hear shooting in the camp, and I am scared and I think of Nyakunde. It only happens at night in the dark, and when I wake up I am scared. The camp is full of noise at night, and sometimes I can't sleep, but it is the shooting that scares me most. My uncle, he was killed in Maribu [also in Ituri] last year also. It is very sad because a lot of people are dead.

My favourite thing in the camp is school – it is very good and I like it very much. We go every day in the afternoon. Other children go in the morning, but we must go later. We play games and we learn things and I like my teacher very much. I also like mangoes, but there are not many mangoes here in Bunia. In my garden in Nyakunde we had a lot of mangoes – it was full of mangoes and we had mango trees in the garden.

My mum, she came to visit us a few days ago here in the camp. I think it was Sunday because there wasn't any school. But we cannot go and live with her in Kindia because she says it is not good for us there. So we must live here with my brother. I miss her very much and I want to see her again soon.

Liberia

Founded in 1847 by slaves freed from the USA, Liberia is a small West African country, bordered by Sierra Leone, Guinea and the Ivory Coast. Liberia means 'land of the free' and its historical connections to the USA are evident both in its flag, which is very similar to the Stars and Stripes, and in the name of its capital, Monrovia, after the American President Monroe.

When the freed slaves returned, they looked down on the indigenous African people. The Americo-Liberians form about five per cent of the population, but they control most of the political power and wealth.

For twenty years now, Liberia has suffered from political instability and violence, culminating in an intense civil war. Over 200,000 people have been killed, and nearly a third of the population has had to flee their homes.

Partly as a result of the constant fighting, Liberia is one of the poorest countries in the world and is in a state of severe crisis. The health system has completely collapsed. This, combined with poor

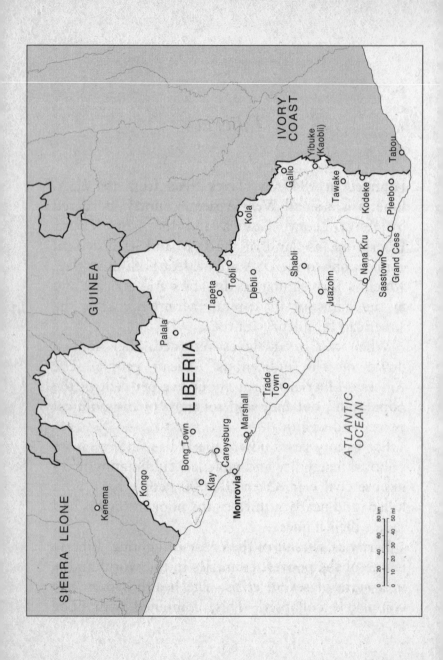

sanitation, means that Liberians are dying of diarrhoea and other curable diseases. HIV/AIDS infection rates have increased during the war. Most schools have been shut down for years, meaning that children are growing up illiterate and un-educated. Many people do not have enough to eat and the economy is in a catastrophic state.

The civil war has also led to increased instability in neighbouring West African countries. As refugees, arms and combatants cross the country's borders, the conflict in Liberia has fuelled vio-lence and unrest in the Ivory Coast and Sierra Leone, and in turn has been intensified by these conflicts.

The causes of the fighting are complex. On the one hand, the wars can be seen as part of a struggle between rival warlords for control of the govern-ment and the country's resources. But the fighting has also been fuelled by a sense of injustice among many ordinary Liberians at the poverty and insecurity in which they have had to live.

As well as causing massive physical damage, the turmoil has undermined Liberian society. Many Liberians have more respect for tribal loyalties than they do for central government, and the warring parties are organized along ethnic rather than political lines. And many children are involved in the fighting; some estimates put the number of child soldiers in Liberia as high as 20,000.

One result of the conflict is that more than 1 million people have been forced into exile either as internally displaced people or as refugees in neighbouring countries, including Guinea, Sierra Leone and the Ivory Coast. These countries themselves suffer from widespread violence and insecurity, and the refugee camps have sometimes been exposed to attack by rebel groups. Conditions in the camps can be tough, yet some Liberian refugees have spent up to ten years (in some cases most of their adult lives) in refugee camps.

In June, July and August 2003 the fighting in Liberia reached new heights of violence. These months are known in Liberia as World War I, World War II and World War III. Since then an international peace agreement has been signed and Liberia currently faces its best chance for peace in twenty years. However, after fourteen years of violence and destruction, the challenges of rehabilitating Liberia and helping the uprooted to return home are immense. Clashes go on and innocent Liberians continue to be killed, maimed, raped and robbed. Here are four stories from children who have been uprooted from their homes to escape the violence.

William Toe is fifteen years old. He fled his home in Liberia to escape from civil war. He is now living in a transit centre outside the town of Tabou on the Ivory Coast, together with 3,500 other refugees.

I was born and grew up in Old Kru Town, a village on the sea not far from the Ivory Coast. My father is a fisherman. I liked where I lived; I used to have a dog called Blacky, who I played with, and lots of friends to play football with. We used to play football on an airstrip not far from my house. I had to leave Blacky and some of my friends behind when I left my home because of the war.

We left at night when there was a lot of shooting and fighting. It was scary. The soldiers took all of my parents' things, which made me angry. We had to walk along the beach for two hours before we reached the border. I felt happy when we arrived in the Ivory Coast because I felt free. There was no more fighting.

Now my home is inside these fences, in the transit centre. I like it here because I live well. The food is good. For lunch I usually eat bread. And at night I sometimes eat rice or bulgur wheat. I like rice. I also like fish – my favourite fish is Grippe. But we don't eat fish in the transit camp.

I have five sisters and one brother. I am the youngest. My brother is the oldest, he's thirty-three. My mother, brother and sisters all live with me in the camp. But my father lives in a nearby town called Soublaké. He is a fisherman there.

Football is my favourite sport, but sometimes I play volleyball and a fun game called *impasse*. I also go to school. I like school. Maths is my favourite subject. When I grow up I want to study maths and be a doctor so I can treat sick people.

My family isn't planning to return to Liberia right away. But I want to return when there is peace because it's my country. Sometimes I wonder if our house is still there and if I will be able to find my friends again.

Wachan Bohlen is six years old. Like William Toe, she left Liberia to escape from the fighting and is now living in the transit centre in Tabou.

I am six years old and I am from a place called Pleebo in Liberia. I had a big house. My family left Pleebo last year because there was fighting. I remember that day. We took a car and drove all day to Tabou. There was plenty of shooting and it was scary because guns can kill. When I'm scared I can be silent and I hide.

I like the transit centre because I can play games here. I play rolling ball. I am good. Once I won. I also like going to school because I can write in a copybook. My favourite subject is French. When I grow up I want to be a doctor so I can take care of my parents when they get sick.

I have two sisters and one brother living with me here. I am the youngest in the family. I like being the youngest because my mother spoils me. My father also lives here with us. I have one sister who is fifteen. She stayed behind in Liberia.

Every morning I wake up and I wash my face and take a bath. Then I wash the dishes before I have breakfast. Usually I eat bulgur wheat. Sometimes I eat rice. I like rice better than bulgur wheat. After eating, I can play with my friends. I have four friends and my best friend is called Bintu.

Someday I want to go back to Liberia because it is my country. It is my home. I don't know when, but someday when there is peace.

Neyi Memunatu is twelve years old and lives in Jembe Refugee Camp in Sierra Leone, together with almost 8,000 other refugees. He comes from Liberia.

My old home in Liberia was all right. We had food and went to school regularly. But then the war started. We left after the rebels devastated and looted my mother's shop. Our home was completely destroyed and most of my people are now dead. I used to have five brothers and four sisters, but during the war three of my brothers and three of my sisters were killed. So now there are just four of us. My father, Mustapha Nyei, was also murdered by the rebels.

My mother is back in Liberia now with my two brothers. But there are no schools functioning there, and no law and order. So I live here in the camp with my aunt and grandmother and go to school every day.

Most of the time it's very hot. When I'm not at school I love playing kickball, baseball, and all sorts of sport. The food is good – I eat bulgur wheat, cassava, rice, banana, corn soy and fish.

I would like to go back to Liberia one day when there is peace there.

Theresa John is fourteen years old. She fled to Sierra Leone following an attack on her village when she was just nine. She now lives in Jimmi Refugee Camp.

I was born in Sorlormba in the eastern part of Liberia. I am fourteen years old now and I am a Kissi. I have five brothers and three sisters.

One evening in August 1999, our village was attacked by armed men. They shot and killed some people. My parents fled with us to the Sierra Leonean border town of Buedu. We walked through the forest in the night to escape from the horror. In Buedu we could not cope with the raging hunger so we moved further into Sierra Leone, to Daru, to look for food. And from there we moved here, to Jimmi Refugee Camp. Here we have a two-bedroomed mud-walled hut with a plastic sheet over it as the roof.

Every day my mother prepares a meal of bulgur wheat or maize meal that our family feeds on like any other refugee family. I sweep in and around our hut every morning. Then I heat some water for my parents so they can bathe, before I go to school. At school or at home, I always play football and *Lappa-Lappa* games with my friends.

I have happy memories of my old life in Liberia. I

Eqleema's family are Afghan refugees now living in Pakistan where she was born. Here she is in her classroom.
(*See page 29*)

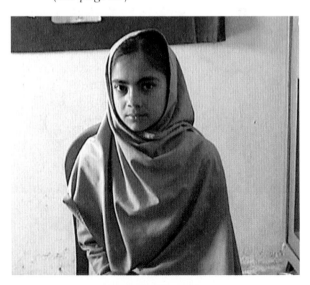

Nadia lives in Pakistan with her family. A refugee from Afghanistan, she misses her old life there.
(*See page 36*)

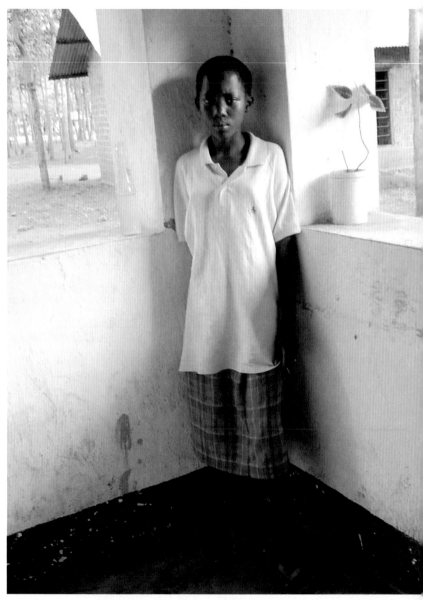

Neema and her family spent two days escaping from Burundi.
They now live in a refugee camp in Tanzania.

(*See page* 95)

Azeza has been living in a deserted school for more than ten years following the destruction of her home during the Iran – Iraq war.
(*See page 47*)

Below: The deserted school where Azeza and her family live.
(*See page 47*)

Martien and his family left Iraq in search of a better life in America.

(*See page 45*)

Merci lives in a refugee camp in the Republic of Congo after she
and her family fled from the Democratic Republic of Congo to
escape from the war.
(*See page 58*)

Desaange and her brother, Innocent, had to flee from their home in the DRC.

(*See page 62*)

Victoria Amina's father was still in a prisoner-of-war camp in Bosnia when she was born in England ten days after her mother arrived as a refugee.
(*See page 19*)

Doruntino and her family left their home in Kosovo when she was four. She still remembers seeing houses being burnt down.
(*See page 11*)

Joyce Ihiju, a refugee from Sudan, now lives in Uganda. 'I find it very painful remembering how my parents were killed in cold blood.'
(*See page 81*)

Alex Obil had to run away from his village in Sudan to escape from the fighting.
(*See page 84*)

can remember having plenty of rice to eat. It makes me sad to think about the way the rebels attacked us and forced us to flee.

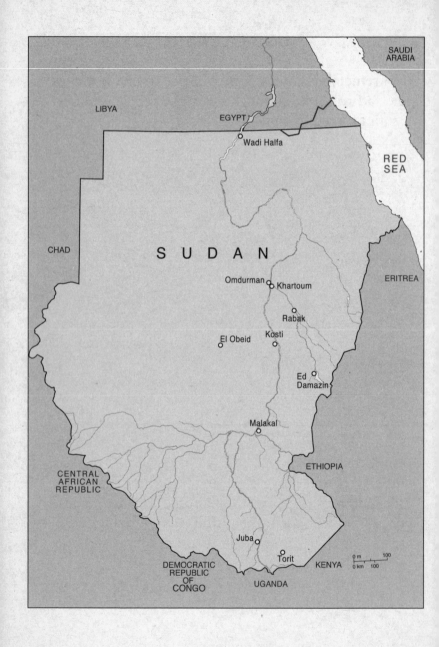

Sudan

Sudan, Africa's largest country, has been the home of many different cultures. Christian kingdoms flourished along the Nile until the sixteenth century. These gave way to Islamic states. In 1889, Britain and Egypt defeated the Sudanese army and ruled the country jointly. The Arab and Muslim north was ruled separately from the African south. Development in the north of the country was favoured over investing in the impoverished south.

Since Sudan's independence in 1956, the country has been devastated by civil war. The discrimination resulted in the emergence of the rebel Sudan People's Liberation Army in the south. The current conflict has been raging since 1983. Over 1.5 million people have died and 4 million have fled their homes to escape the fighting. The war is still primarily between the Arab-dominated government in Khartoum, the capital city, and the ethnically African peoples from the south.

However, the war has also involved conflict among different rebels and between various militias and tribal groups. It is partly about politics, religion and ethnic loyalty, but it is also a struggle for control of the country's vast natural resources – oil, fertile land and water – which are located primarily in the south.

The Sudanese population and economy are in chaos. Schools, hospitals, roads and other essential services have either been destroyed by heavy fighting or have been ruined by a lack of investment due to military expenditures. The displacement of people has interrupted farming cycles and disrupted the provision of social services, creating massive humanitarian need.

Around 200,000 South Sudanese have fled across the border to Uganda. However, the northern regions of Uganda are themselves suffering from armed conflict, especially in the district of Acholiland where the rebel Lord's Resistance Army (LRA) has been fighting the Ugandan government since 1986. The LRA has ruthlessly attacked ordinary people, burning villages, stealing crops and household possessions, laying landmines, ambushing vehicles, attacking women and girls, and killing, maiming and kidnapping adults and children as young as seven. It is estimated that almost half the fighters in the LRA are kidnapped children, and as many as 20,000 children have been abducted since the conflict began. They are forced to endure tremendous hardship. Children are often forced to kill their own family members and destroy their homes and villages. Younger children are preferred because they are intimidated and indoctrinated more easily. Girls are given to rebel commanders as wives. Living conditions are extremely harsh, and many children die of dehydration and hunger.

Sudanese refugees fleeing to Acholiland and neighbouring districts live in crowded camps, such as Kiryandongo and Acholi-pii. They are dependent on the limited assistance provided by the Ugandan government and international organizations.

Since July 2002 the major warring groups in Sudan have been engaged in a peace process which has created a much more secure and stable environment. The political process is reaching its final stages, but the challenge of making peace a reality for the millions of ordinary people in Sudan is only just beginning.

In spring 2004 a major humanitarian crisis occurred in the Darfur region of Western Sudan in which up to a million people were displaced

Here are stories from two young refugees living in camps in Uganda, one from a Southern Sudanese child who is now living in Khartoum in order to escape the fighting and deprivation that plague his home village, and one from a Sudanese living in Kenya.

Joyce Ihiju is fourteen years old and a Sudanese refugee living in Uganda. She left Sudan to escape from the civil war there. Her parents were killed when she was four.

I come from a small village called Torit. I am an only child but we had other relatives living with us, and my parents loved me very much. I miss all of that now.

My father was a driver for one of the local hospitals. My mother was a farmer and used to spend most of her time in the field looking after the crops. I can remember how we only stayed in our house during the day. At night we would hide from the Sudanese People's Liberation Army in the bush or forests. When I was four, disaster struck my family when my father and two of our relatives were ambushed and killed. A few days after my father died, the fighting got worse. My mother started to worry about us staying in the village because anyone found there could be beaten and killed, so we left Torit. But as we fled we were ambushed. My mother was grabbed, seriously beaten and killed by the rebels. I was beaten too, but a woman helped me to escape.

We ran to someone's house, where I lived for quite a while (I don't remember exactly how long).

But then that home was also attacked by rebels and burned down. I managed to escape and ran to another household, who took me in on the condition that I did not stay for too long. I lived with that family for about three months, before finding another family to look after me. I stayed with them until we fled to Uganda to escape from the fighting. There we were taken in by the Acholi-pii Refugee Camp. But when the camp was attacked by the Lords Resistance Army we had to move here to Kiryandongo Refugee Camp. My early memories of this camp are happy. For the first time I felt peace of mind and regained my hope for the future.

But then my foster family grew tired of me and asked me to leave. So I had to manage on my own until another 'Good Samaritan' family offered to look after me. Although I have a new family now, my life has not changed much. I feel lonely and afraid of doing anything that might annoy my 'new parents'. I live with six other orphans and I'm not sure of my next destination or what will happen to me tomorrow. I spend all my time doing lots of housework and gardening and I have no time for playing. By the end of the day my body is aching and I am exhausted. During the last six months my foster father has started to be sarcastic to me, which makes me feel like it's time to find another place to stay where I can be free like other children.

Whenever I'm asked about my family life and background, I burst into tears before saying anything. I find it very painful, remembering how my parents were killed in cold blood, and the only way to release the pain is to cry. My greatest wish is to find my relatives and get resettled.

Alex Obil is thirteen years old and is a member of the Lokoya tribe. He left Sudan for Uganda when he was nine to escape the civil war. His mother died of an illness when he was very young.

I still remember the day my father was killed during a tribal clash. After that, my elder brother and sister looked after me. But seven years later we were separated when we had to run away from our village to escape from the fighting.

It took a week of walking without food, water or rest to reach Uganda. I left my sister and brothers behind and now I don't know whether they are alive or dead. I have no hope of meeting them again unless it is God's wish.

I spent my first two years in Uganda staying in Adjumnani. Life there was very tough; I did not have the right documentation so had to depend entirely on casual work to survive. It was so bad that sometimes I thought going back to die in Sudan would be better than suffering in a foreign country.

But after two years I moved here to the Kiryandongo Refugee Settlement. Now I live with a foster family; they are good to me and I am grateful for everything they've done for me. Finding some-one to take care of me after being on my own was a wonderful moment. Although my foster mother is kind, she is too poor to pay for everything I need, especially my school fees. So I find work whenever I can to earn some money to buy school books and pay for my schooling. And when I have time, I play football with my school friends.

I still remember how, when we lived in Sudan, life was good. My sister loved me very much and took care of me. Although I could not enjoy the taste of having a mother, my sister became a true mother to me. I'll never forget the day my father was shot during a tribal clash.

I worry about who will take care of me if my present foster mother sends me away. How will I survive? One day I'd like to return to Sudan so I can help people at home. I know they are still suffering.

Moses Okumu John lives in Haj Yousif, a Squatter Camp in north Khartoum, Sudan's capital. An internally displaced person from the war-ravaged south of Sudan, his family sent him to the capital to find a better education. He is twelve years old.

Life of an 'internally displaced person' in Khartoum

My name is Moses Okumu John and I was born in Juba in the south of Sudan. My father, John Ochan, works for the Juba National Electricity Corporation and he has two wives. My mother is his first. When I was eight years old, I moved to Khartoum and I now live in Haj Yousif. Every day, we have to walk far from our homes to find water, and there is little electricity or health clinics in the camp.

I started going to school when I still lived in Juba but the schools there were very bad. There were not enough books and chairs for the students, and the teachers knew very little. So my family sent me to Khartoum to find a better school.

Since arriving here four years ago, I haven't been back to Juba to see my mother, brothers and sisters. Sometimes my father comes to Khartoum for his work. He also comes to see his second wife, my stepmother, who takes care of me. Even though she is not my mother, she treats me well and loves me, and I like her. Nine people live in the same home as me; they are part of my second mother's family: five women and four men. But I still miss my real family – my three sisters and two brothers – who are still in Juba. I would very much like to go to see them.

For me, though, life in Khartoum is better than life in Juba. I've been very lucky because I go to a good Catholic school with excellent teachers and enough supplies. In Juba, many of the students had to leave school because their families did not have enough money to pay the fees. My father gets paid, but he often has to wait two or three months for his salary. I am also glad that in Khartoum there is enough food to eat. In Juba the food is too expensive for many people and they go hungry. And often food supplies cannot reach Juba at all because of the war. Families here in Khartoum eat two or three times each day, usually *fuul masir*, green vegetables, meat and rice. Back in Juba we only ate once a day.

If I could be anything, I would like to be a doctor if all goes well with my education.

John Chol Kon is a Sudanese refugee living in Kenya. He was so young when he left his home that he didn't understand why he had to flee. But he remembers the events as if they were yesterday.

That night I was not in our home, I was staying with my friend, some distance from our house. I had been allowed to go and visit my friend. It had been a normal day and we had spent the day playing with other boys since we were too young to do anything else.

But that night was not to be a normal night. We heard sounds of so many bullets and immediately realized that there was serious fighting. We were very terrified and began crying with much fear. My friend's parents took us out and we began running in a very confused way. In the process, I lost my friend and his parents and found myself in the company of another family, who allowed me to join them. I was only five when I had to leave my home and I haven't seen my parents again. I don't know why my village was attacked, but I have heard that the government of Sudan, which is very strong, has been fighting with our leader. They have killed many of our people and they still continue to do that.

For many days after that night we kept on

walking through many places that I could not recognize. We went without food and sometimes had no water to drink. Sometimes I would cry for a long time.

After a long time we arrived in a refugee camp called Kakuma in Kenya, where I found one of my uncles. I have been living here with him for ten years now. I often get lonely and my life would be much better if my mother and father were with me. My uncle isn't as interested in me as they would be. He isn't very active in looking after me. I've heard that there may be peace one day in Sudan and I want to go back there to meet my parents. I believe that one day we will be reunited.

When we came to the camp in 1994, we used to be provided with enough food. But since 1996 things have changed. We get very little food; sometimes we only get a little maize, which is not enough for the family. We are expected to use our own money to buy extra food, but where do we get the money?

Safety is a big concern. We live in constant fear of armed criminals who for a long time have made life difficult for the refugees. Some have been killed during clashes with local people.

I also worry about all the children in the camp who have to work. Children get involved in brick-making, either to sell or to help build their family's shelters. But mostly children are sent to fetch water in heavy jerrycans. I don't think this is good for them.

I do go to school in the camp. This year I will take my final exams, but there are not enough textbooks so I don't know if I will ever be able to realize my dream of returning to Sudan as a big professor of education.

Burundi

For most of the first half of the last century Burundi, along with its neighbour Rwanda, was ruled by Belgium. The territories were known as Ruanda-Urundi until independence in 1962 resulted in Urundi becoming a separate country, Burundi. Since then, divisions between ethnic groups, exploited during the long years of colonial rule, have plagued the country: the Tutsis who, although they make up only 14 per cent of the population, have always been more dominant, and the Hutu majority.

Since 1993 alone, Burundi's civil conflict is thought to have claimed over 300,000 lives and displaced an estimated 1 million people. Ongoing tensions between the Hutu and Tutsi communities erupted with the October 1993 assassination of President Melchior Ndadaye in a Tutsi-led *coup d'état*. The murder of Ndadaye, a Hutu and the nation's first democratically elected head of state, sparked political and ethnic violence that left nearly 100,000 Burundians dead, and it triggered a massive refugee influx into Tanzania, as well as

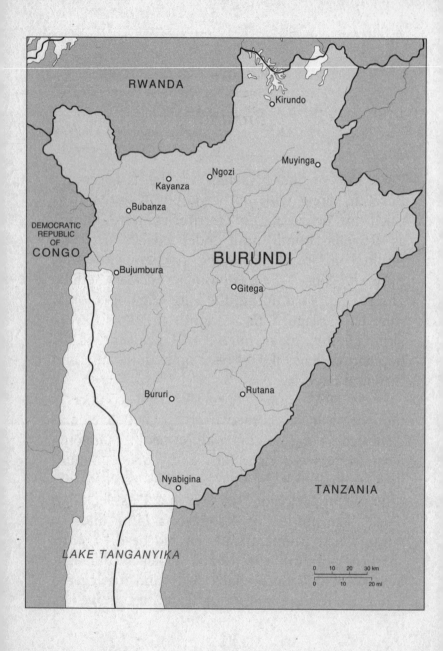

RWANDA

Kirundo

Muyinga

Ngozi

Kayanza

Bubanza

DEMOCRATIC
REPUBLIC
OF
CONGO

BURUNDI

Bujumbura

Gitega

Bururi

Rutana

Nyabigina

TANZANIA

LAKE TANGANYIKA

0   10   20   30 km

0   10   20 mi

neighbouring countries. The crisis in Burundi was a grim prelude to the chaos that would overtake the region with the Rwandan genocide in 1994, when over 800,000 Tutsis and politically moderate Hutus were killed, and over 500,000 survivors sought refuge in the camps of western Tanzania. The death of Burundi's interim president, Cyprien Ntaryamira, in the plane crash that instigated the Rwandan genocide destabilized Burundi still further.

The political and ethnic clashes reached their peak in 1996, when the Burundian armed forces' commander-in-chief, Pierre Buyoya, seized power in a military coup, precipitating yet another wave of Burundian refugees into Tanzania.

In early 2004, Tanzania was hosting approximately 500,000 refugees within its borders, the vast majority from Burundi and the Democratic Republic of Congo. Tanzania is also home to over 300,000 Burundians who, despite having fled their country of origin, lack official refugee status. This group is dispersed throughout the local population. Despite promising developments in Burundi, violence and civil strife persist. The peaceful political transition from a Tutsi to a Hutu president in April 2003; comprehensive peace agreements between the transitional government and the main rebel faction, CNDD-FDD, in late 2003 and early 2004; and the decision by the African Union monitoring force to extend its peacekeeping mission in Burundi until May 2004, when it has urged the deployment of United Nations troops, have all contributed to a wary optimism among those familiar with the conflict. Scepticism abounds, however, and it is far from certain when the ongoing fighting will come to a complete end. Here are two young Burundians' very different stories about how they found themselves to be refugees.

Neema Ndayihimbaze is thirteen and has lived in a refugee camp in Tanzania for seven years since leaving her home in Burundi.

My name is Neema Ndayihimbaze. I am thirteen years old, and for the past seven years I have lived in Nduta Refugee Camp. My father is Biryanguze Ezironi, and my mother is Ndamukemanye Justine. I have six sisters and one brother. Two of my sisters are older than I am: Mpawemayo Emeline is seventeen, and Niyibikora Joseline is fifteen. My brother, Kwizera Seth, is eleven. My other sisters are also younger than I am. Niyogushimwa Nepola is nine, Nimemya Fauziya is seven, Nshimirimama Daimess is five, and Tuyisenge Elda is three.

Before we came here, our lives were very different. We are Burundians. Our village was called Nyabigina. We were all born there and had never lived anywhere else. It was our home. When I think of it now, I always think of our house. It was a very good house, with white walls, a room for each of us, and a kitchen. We also had a small house on our property for my father's younger brother. The best thing of all was our television. I *loved* to watch our television. We kept it outside our house, and there were so many of us who used to watch in the evenings – the neighbours would come to watch, and my parents, my sisters and brother, my uncle, and all our friends. Sometimes it felt as though there were a hundred people, all sitting together and watching and enjoying it. We used to watch football all the time and dramas, like a programme on Burundian television called *Ninde*. One story on *Ninde* that I particularly remember was about a girl who loved a young man, and who agreed to marry him. But when the day of the wedding arrived, the girl discovered that her fiancé was a thief who had stolen livestock from another family in the village, so he was taken away to prison. We used to see people on the television, leaders and politicians in other parts of Burundi, and we saw that the world was very large, and there was much to know. Our television is the thing that I miss the most.

Besides watching television, I used to love to eat in our old house. My mother would cook for us in the kitchen, and we would all eat together outside. My sisters and brother and I would eat in one group, with friends and neighbours who had stopped by. My parents and uncle would eat in a separate group nearby. My mother would cook rice, beans, banana, and all kinds of meat. I especially loved eating rice and meat together. Those times were lovely.

I used to love going to school. I always wanted to study, because I knew that it would give me a good future; I wanted to be a teacher or a nurse when I was older, so I enjoyed my lessons. We used to go to school at 8.00 in the morning, then come home at noon for lunch, before going back again. In the evenings, after school, I would play with my friends, especially my three closest friends, Furaha, Riziki and Francine. One of our favourite games was called *ola*: two girls stood facing each other, tossing a ball back and forth, with one girl between them who had to dodge the ball. We also used to play *ola umusenyi*. It was like *ola*, except that when the ball went out of bounds, one of the girls would fill a bottle with sand. Whoever managed to fill the bottle three times was the winner.

Our life in Nyabigina was peaceful and happy until the war came to the village. The trouble first began when our President Ndadaye was killed. When the violence broke out, my family and I fled. We walked to a village called Rusoro, which was a two-day journey away, across the border in Tanzania. We thought we would be safer there than in Nyabigina. It was very frantic on the way to Rusoro. I was running in the street when, suddenly, I collided with a bicycle. It was an extremely forceful and violent crash, and even though it happened over ten years ago, I still have the scar on my leg. The whole experience was very painful, and it upsets me when I think about it.

We remained in Rusoro for two weeks, and then decided to go back home. But things were never completely safe in Nyabigina after that. Every time the fighting drew near, we would have to flee into the bush for the night, because it was too dangerous to stay in the house. We had to separate, and I still remember how frightened we were. My mother and my brother and sisters and I would spend the night deep in the bush, far from the house, but my father would not be with us; he would stay near the house to make sure it was safe. In the morning, we would all return home together.

Things stayed like this for the next four years, until finally life in Nyabigina became too dangerous. The young men of the village were involved in the fighting, and my parents felt that it was impossible for us to stay. My father held a family meeting one evening, and he insisted that we must leave because the situation had become so bad. My uncle had just got married and did not want to leave Nyabigina, but the rest of us agreed with my parents.

When we woke up the next morning, the road in front of the house was filled with people; families from Nyabigina and Ruviyagira (a village that was further away) were fleeing before our eyes. As soon as we saw them, we decided that we should join them. We took food, cooking pots, clothing, money, and our television, and began walking.

The journey to the Tanzanian border took two days. Although we had enough food for the trip, water was very scarce. We spent the night in the bush, trying to hide from the armed soldiers and bandits who were patrolling everywhere. My parents warned us all to be silent so that we would not be found; none of us was allowed to talk. Even during the day we didn't speak much. My parents made us walk in front of them so that they could watch us, and they carried all our possessions so that we children would not be burdened. But because the eight of us were not speaking to one another, we could hear clearly what our parents were saying. They kept asking each other where we would live, and how we would live there, and what would happen to all of us when we crossed the border.

When we reached the border, two days later, we found a group of rebel fighters assembled there. They demanded 1,000 francs per family in order to cross. Luckily we were able to pay, so we arrived in Tanzania without any problems. After crossing, we walked for two hours until we reached Rusoro, the same village we had gone to four years earlier, when all the trouble began. We were among the first group of refugees to arrive in Rusoro, and so we were welcomed. The villagers showed us where we would all sleep. We left all our possessions with a family in the village and they said they would watch them. When we came back three hours later, we discovered that one of our cooking pots was gone. We all decided to stay quiet about it. They were Tanzanians, and we were foreigners staying in their country, so we knew that our word would not be taken seriously if we accused them of theft. We began to learn Kiswahili, and within about two weeks we could communicate with the villagers.

Our situation in Rusoro was really very bad. There was not enough food. Even though we would buy what food we could, it was still not enough. We had to sell our television, which was very hard. My sisters and brother and I could not go to school. And there was absolutely nothing to do. Even though we made friends with the Tanzanian families in the village, we were still idle. My parents had nothing to do either. In Nyabigina, my mother was a farmer and my father worked as a builder, but in Rusoro they could do nothing. That was when we decided to enter the camp. We had stayed in Rusoro for two months and conditions were very hard, so we hoped that life in the camp would be easier.

We have been in Nduta now since 1997. There are eleven of us in total: my parents, my sisters and brother and me, and our cousin, Tumaini Edmond, who is five years old. Our cousin joined us after we arrived in Nduta. His father had been killed, and his mother had remarried in the camp, but her new family objected to Tumaini because he was the child of her previous marriage. So now he lives with us as our youngest brother. My uncle who stayed behind in Nyabigina is dead. He was killed by soldiers while trying to hide inside one of the houses in the village.

All eleven of us live in a brick house with three rooms: two for sleeping and one for eating. The roof is two pieces of plastic sheeting. We have lived here since we first arrived in Nduta, but none of us feels safe. Last August, the whole family was asleep, but because it was raining heavily my mother came into our room to check up on us. When she entered our room, she saw that the window had been completely destroyed, and when she looked around she realized that a plastic basin was missing. Thieves had broken the window and taken things from our home. We were terrified.

The next night, the thieves came again. This time, they entered through another window. My parents woke up when they felt something tugging on the mosquito net above their bed, and they gave chase, but they were not fast enough. This time, the thieves took our clothes, our cooking pots and utensils, and our camera. They also took our peace of mind, because none of us could sleep for many nights afterwards. I tried to spend as much time as I could at school and with friends, because I didn't want to stay in the house. Even now, six months later, I am still afraid. I find myself wondering whether one day all of us will be killed. We keep hearing rumours that the thieves will return and destroy our home, and our neighbours are always threatening us.

Despite everything that's happened, I have kept up with my studies. I began school immediately after arriving in Nduta. I still want to become a teacher or a nurse; I see others in the camp, and those who are educated have a good life. This has helped me to stay determined. I want that life when I am older, though I wonder how it will happen in the midst of so much trouble.

During my holidays I go with my parents to look for firewood, but in the evenings during the week I am usually free. I try and spend time with my friends, and we play different games together. One of the games we play is *kombolewa*, where someone throws a ball, and while one person runs to get it, the others all scatter and hide. The person who ran for the ball then has to find everyone. Furaha, Riziki and Francine, my three closest friends from Nyabigina, were also in Nduta until recently. Furaha and Riziki repatriated to Burundi three months ago, and Francine's family has settled in a village in Tanzania called Ntongwe, near Lake Tanganyika. I have other friends in Nduta, but none as close as they were.

In Nduta, we thought life would be safe, because the war was far away. We thought there would be no fighting and insecurity like there was when we left Nyabigina. But life here is becoming impossible for us. The hardest thing is the food shortage. There is never enough to eat. I usually eat beans and maize paste mixed with cotton oil. There is no fruit, and there are no bananas. We usually have two meals a day, one at midday and one in the evening. Also, the rainy season here is full of problems. In Nyabigina the soil was sandy, so we had no trouble when it rained. Here, the rainy season turns everything into mud, and it is very difficult to live. No matter what the weather, we cannot get *anything* that we need, whether it's food, clothing, shoes, cooking materials, or other things. The deprivation is such a hardship. As a refugee, you cannot get the things you need to live your life. There is just no way.

My greatest wish used to be to return home to my old good life. But lately I've become afraid that, whether we stay or go back, our lives will not improve. Life would be so good if we were in another country, with no war, and no thieves, and no one to threaten us. But I have begun to worry that Burundi will be unsafe for us, and that our lives will be endangered there. My father was one of eleven brothers, but all ten of my uncles were killed in the war. Those who have returned to Burundi pass messages back to those of us still in the camps, and we were told that if my father returns, he will be killed as well. So what kind of life will we go back to? Our lives were good there once, but will they be again? If we stay here in the camps, we will continue to hear gunfire at night, to live in fear of thieves, to be threatened by our neighbours. There is no peace for us, either here or there. I do not see a solution.

Shirley Iraganje is ten. She's from Burundi and now lives in Phoenix, Arizona, USA.

My name is Shirley Iraganje. I was born on 8 July 1994 in a small but beautiful country called Burundi in the Great Lakes region of Central Africa.

When I was living in Burundi I had a lot of friends and family that I really miss now. I remember an aunt of mine telling me that I had to stay with her for a while because my dad was 'working' far from our home and my mum had to stay at school. Now I know that we were living separately so that we would not get killed together. My little brother did not stop crying because he was missing our parents so much. I remember I saw my dad again when he was taking us to a plane and I asked him: 'Where have you been?' The only answer he gave me was: *'Vite, vite! On va rater l'avion!!'* ['Hurry, hurry, we're about to miss the flight!!'] We were joining with our mother, who had already left the country.

I was four when we left. I remember leaving behind me a nice house I was living in. There were lots of different flowers all around it. It was next to a mountain, and my aunt and myself used to climb at sunset, her carrying me on her back. I still miss her. The flight to Burkina Faso was very long. Worse! Dad was not coming with us. The following day I do not know if I was excited or angry to see my mother again. I asked her the same question: 'Why did you leave us by ourselves?' I was only four then so I couldn't understand her answer, but I do now.

A few months later my dad joined us. I don't know where he had been. Then we moved from a studio into a very small, one-bedroom apartment. During that time my father was trying to find a job while my mother went to school. He found a job in a French high school as a teacher. Later on I went to the same school. Two years to wait until I am six. Meanwhile another journey was pointing ahead.

It was one evening in September. A friend of ours in military uniform took us to the airport of Ouagadougou in Burkina Faso. We changed planes three times. At the end of the journey in Phoenix, Arizona, somebody was waiting for us and took us to a hotel, where we spent the first night. The following day we were settling into a one-bedroom apartment. A year later, my family moved again. But it was still in the same apartment complex, only in an apartment that had two bedrooms. Two months later, my brother Ralph and I started going to school. After two years in America my baby brother was born. His name is Robert Comblé Baransaka. Then we moved again into a three-bedroom house in Peoria [also in Arizona], where we live now. My dad used to call it our small 'White House' with red and green curtains, my mother's favourite colours. It has a backyard. My brothers and I are happy that we have somewhere to run around and play all kinds of games.

Today I attend a school called Cotton Boll Elementary. My teacher was proud of me because at the end of the first grade I received an award letter signed President Clinton. I was also student of the month in my old school. Last year I won so many honours I was chosen out of my whole class to win a bike. When I heard, I was so excited. My parents were very proud of me and I was proud of myself too. I'm a member of a girls' basketball team. Our coach is a great person. We took a picture that I keep in front of my bed by my computer so that I can see it every morning.

I dream of being wealthy enough to buy a big house for my parents when they are old and avoid them having to spend the rest of their days in a nursing care home centre.

At home I help my mother cook and clean. When

my dad and my mum are at work I help my aunt and neighbour take care of my two little brothers. Sometimes they make me mad because they're always screaming and running around and messing around, and the worst part about it is that I have to clean up after them when doing my homework. They always make a mess, no matter what they're doing, but I'll always love them. Whenever I have free time to myself I go to my room and take out a book and read. I love reading so much. I have tons of books. I like mystery, scary or adventure books. I'll always read even when I get older. I would like to write a book telling the world about my sad memories: about how I left my friends behind me, maybe forever, because I do not know whether or not they have been killed meanwhile.

I remember when I was still in Africa, and the war was going on. My mum told me that her father got killed when my mum was just a little girl, that's how long the war has been going on. Myself, I became a refugee when I was still very young. When we moved here I was very nervous about starting a new school and a new life.

My mother is teaching me how to cook. I love the kind of dishes she makes using groceries she buys from the African and the Manilla markets. Also I adore pizza. The smell of pizza reminds me of those small pieces of bread we used to eat with fresh milk at breakfast every morning in Bujumbura. This is the story about my life.

Glossary

asylum seeker	someone who has left his or her home country and asks for refugee status
atrocities	evil acts
beignets	fried squares of dough
biological weapons	living organisms used purposefully to hurt others, e.g. disease
cassava	the edible root of a perennial woody shrub
chemical weapons	artificial substances used purposefully to hurt others, e.g. nerve gas, such as Zyxlon B or Sarin
civil war	a conflict between people of the same country
combatant	someone who fights during a conflict
coup	aggressive attack to seize power from government
Dari	one of the official languages of Afghanistan

deployment	the movement of soldiers or combatants into position for warring action
destabilize	upset a secure or balanced environment
displaced people	those who have to leave their homes due to unrest or violence
ethnic cleansing	the massacre of an ethnic group by people from another ethnic group
ethnic group	a group of people with the same cultural or national traditions
extremist	someone with a fanatical opinion, who might consider violent action acceptable to further their cause
faction	a group forming part of a bigger one
fuul masir	a bean staple in Sudan
genocide	the purposeful murder of a group of people, usually of the same race
ghetto	an area of a city, usually occupied by a minority group living in poverty
humanitarian	that which provides for human welfare
indoctrinated	when a group or individual has been convinced or taught to accept a certain way of thinking

injustice	when something is unfair
interim	in the meantime
internally displaced people (IDPs)	people who have fled their homes but are still living within the borders of their own country
manioc	see *cassava*
militia	informal rebel forces
monitoring	watching
paramilitary	unofficial armed force
Pashto	one of the official languages of Afghanistan
pledge	promise
Qur'an	the Islamic sacred book, believed to be the word of God as dictated to Muhammad by the archangel Gabriel
rally	protest march
reconstruction	the rebuilding of
refugee	someone who has had to flee from their home country to escape a natural disaster, or persecution, or war
regime	the ruling power
rehabilitate	to restore

repatriate	to return someone to their home country
republic	a country with a head of state elected by its citizens
sanctions	action taken by a country to persuade another country to change its policies, e.g. restrictions of trade
sanctuary	a safe place
sanitation	public health systems, e.g. provision of drinking water
suppress	to stop or prevent
transitional	relating to a time of change
warlord	leader of an aggressive force

Acknowledgements

We would like to thank the IRC staff and personnel who have participated directly in this project and many others who are too numerous to mention.

OFFICE	PERSON
DRC	Werner Vasant
Iraq	Denis Dragovic, Maytham Mohammad, Fadi Fadel
Ivory Coast	Martin Hayes, Magali Chelpi
Kenya	Kelly Williams, Elijah Okeyo, Jason Phillips
Pakistan	Pilar Robledo, Naomi Reich, Helay Zadran, Chin Chin
RoC	Julie R. Dargis, Gang Karume, Aaron Rippenkroegger
Sierra Leone	Noah Ochola, David Gatare
Sudan	Addison Thompson, Semir Tanovic
Tanzania	Maha Hussain, Michael Amanya
Uganda	Ciarán Donnelly, Kurt Tjossem

OFFICE	PERSON
UK	Christine Oram, George Graham, Mike Young, Alyoscia D'Onofrio
USA	Cindy Jensen, Bob Montgomery, Robin de Marcos
Non-IRC	Abedin Bajraktari, Lilijan Sulejmanovic

The stories in this book (with the exception of Doruntino and Victoria) have been told by children who are participating in programmes run by International Rescue Committee (IRC).

INTERNATIONAL RESCUE COMMITTEE UK

Founded in 1933, the International Rescue Committee is among the world's leading humanitarian agencies providing relief, rehabilitation, protection, resettlement services and advocacy for refugees, displaced persons and victims of oppression and violent conflict.

Currently working in some twenty-five countries, the IRC distributes lifesaving aid, rebuilds shattered communities, establishes schools, trains teachers, cares for war-traumatized children, rehabilitates health systems, restores lost livelihoods and strengthens the capacity of local organizations and institutions.

For more information, visit www.the IRC.org.

Wherever or whenever war breaks out the lives of children are touched and often changed. Here are some more books you might like to read that give us some understanding about what it is like to live in a country at war:

Non-fiction

Zlata Filipović
Zlata's Diary
0140374639

Zlata started her diary in 1991 when she was living in Sarajevo, in what was then called Yugoslavia. She was eleven years old and was living a settled life until 5 April 1992 when she wrote, *'Something is going on in town. You can hear gunfire from the hills...'* The war that was breaking Yugoslavia apart had reached Sarajevo and Zlata's diary records her feelings alongside the events of the war.

Anne Frank
The Diary of a Young Girl
0141315180

Perhaps the most famous of all wartime diaries – Anne's record of life in hiding in Amsterdam during World War II touches the hearts of every generation. Her diary tells of the War and the persecution of the Jewish people. But alongside these huge events are her thoughts and feelings about growing up – so her story is of a very real girl growing up in terrible times.

Carol Ann Lee
Anne Frank's Story
0141309261

ANNE FRANK'S STORY goes beyond Anne's famous diary. It follows Anne from her birth in Germany through to her happy childhood in Amsterdam, the two years she and her family spent in hiding from the Nazis and their imprisonment and eventual death in the concentration camps.

Thura Al-Windawi
Thura's Diary
0141317698

Thura is an Iraqi teenager living in Baghdad when the bombs begin to fall in 2003. Suddenly her ordinary life is in turmoil, normality disappears and the future is uncertain. Thura finds the act of recording events and feelings somehow calms her and helps her to cope. Her story about the effects of war could be the story of a whole generation of Iraqi children.

Barry Turner
One Small Suitcase
0141314699

An account of the *Kindertransport* children – the children brought from Nazi Germany in the 1930s to start new lives in England. The children's comments are powerful and at times emotional. Barry Turner's words tell the story of up to ten thousand refugee children who faced a future without their families.

Novels:

Carrie's War
Nina Bawden
0140306897

Carrie and her brother Nick were evacuees from London during World War II. Unlike refugees who often have to leave their homes forever, their exile was temporary, just until the bombing stopped. This is not a story of the war but a story of children away from home and of events that affect them forever.

Boy Overboard
Morris Gleitzman
014131625X

Jamal and his sister, Bibi, have to leave their home and the life they know in Afghanistan and take an incredible journey in search of a new life in Australia. Their story is of adventure, football, friendship, hope and survival and is the story of many families who find themselves on the wrong side of a political argument. This is a great book – a mix of humour, real life and fear.

The Other Side of Truth
Beverley Naidoo
0141304766

This story starts with a terrible tragedy as Sade and her brother Femi see their mother shot dead on their doorstep, attacked because their father, a journalist, has dared to write the truth. They must leave Nigeria to be safe and they must leave alone for a life in England that begins by being as full of fear as the life they have left behind. This is a strong, moving book about big things like justice and freedom. Femi and Sade's story is continued in *Web of Lies*, 0141314664.

Tell the Moon to Come Out
Joan Lingard
0141316896

During the Spanish Civil War in the 1930s, Nick travels from Scotland in search of his father who went to fight in Spain three years earlier — and never returned. Spain is dangerous, full of secrets and it's hard to know who to trust, but Nick doesn't give up. This novel tells of the effects of war but is a story of love and adventure too.

Goodnight Mister Tom
Michelle Magorian
0140315411

An amazing novel about evacuation in World War II that seldom leaves readers dry-eyed. Willie Beech is a sad, deprived child and his growing relationship with Tom Oakley teaches him something of trust and love. This story reads like a piece of history, so real that you can't help but be changed by it.

Michelle Magorian also wrote *Back Home* (0140319077), the story of a girl evacuated from England to the USA. Rusty's story shows how hard it was for evacuees to settle down again at home after so much had happened to them — she's a tough character, exciting to read about.